Before the First Word
The Poetry of Lorna Crozier

Before the First Word
The Poetry of Lorna Crozier

Selected
with an
introduction by
Catherine Hunter
and an
afterword by
Lorna Crozier

lps LAURIER POETRY SERIES

Wilfrid Laurier University Press

We acknowledge the support of the Canada Council for the Arts for our publishing program. We acknowledge the financial support of the Government of Canada through the Book Publishing Industry Development Program for our publishing activities.

ONTARIO ARTS COUNCIL
CONSEIL DES ARTS DE L'ONTARIO

Library and Archives Canada Cataloguing in Publication

Crozier, Lorna, 1948–

   Before the first word : the poetry of Lorna Crozier / selected, with an introduction by Catherine Hunter ; and an afterword by Lorna Crozier.

(Laurier poetry series)
Includes bibliographical references.
ISBN 0-88920-489-6

   I. Hunter, Catherine, 1957–   II. Title.   III. Series.

PS8555.R72A6 2005   C811'.54   C2005-904701-1

© 2005 Wilfrid Laurier University Press
Waterloo, Ontario, Canada N2L 3C5
www.wlupress.wlu.ca

Cover image: Erica Grimm Vance. *Growing Fiery Wings*, 1998. Encaustic, steel, and gold, 35" x 45". The artist's work can be seen at www.egrimmvance.com

Cover and text design by P. J. Woodland.

Table of Contents

Foreword

At the beginning of the twenty-first century, poetry in Canada—writing and publishing it, reading and thinking about it—finds itself in a strangely conflicted place. We have many strong poets continuing to produce exciting new work, and there is still a small audience for poetry; but increasingly, poetry is becoming a vulnerable art, for reasons that don't need to be rehearsed.

But there are things to be done: we need more real engagement with our poets. There needs to be more access to their work in more venues—in classrooms, in the public arena, in the media—and there needs to be more, and more different kinds of publications, that make the wide range of our contemporary poetry more widely available.

The hope that animates this new series from Wilfrid Laurier University Press is that these volumes will help to create and sustain the larger readership that contemporary Canadian poetry so richly deserves. Like our fiction writers, our poets are much celebrated abroad; they should just as properly be better known at home.

Our idea has been to ask a critic (sometimes herself a poet) to select thirty-five poems from across a poet's career; write an engaging, accessible introduction; and have the poet write an afterword. In this way, we think that the usual practice of teaching a poet through eight or twelve poems from an anthology will be much improved upon; and readers in and out of classrooms will have more useful, engaging, and comprehensive introductions to a poet's work. Readers might also come to see more readily, we hope, the connections among, as well as the distances between, the life and the work.

It was the ending of an Al Purdy poem that gave Margaret Laurence the epigraph for *The Diviners*: "but they had their being once / and left a place to stand on." Our poets still do, and they are leaving many places to stand on. We hope that this series will help, variously, to show how and why this is so.

—*Neil Besner*
General Editor

Biographical Note

One of Canada's best-known poets, Lorna Crozier was born in Swift Current, Saskatchewan, on May 24, 1948, and grew up there, moving to Saskatoon after high school to attend the University of Saskatchewan. After graduating with a BA in 1969, she returned to Swift Current to teach high school English. Her first books of poetry, *Inside Is the Sky* (1976) and *Crow's Black Joy* (1978), established Crozier as a poet intimately familiar not only with a prairie landscape but, just as importantly, with the climate of feeling generated on the prairie. In the seventies, Crozier was involved in many of the movements that began to establish Saskatchewan writing as a strong force in Canada, including the founding of the Summer School of the Arts at Fort San, the start of the Saskatchewan Writers' Guild, and the founding of two important literary journals, *Grain* and *Salt*.

In 1978 Crozier began to live with poet Patrick Lane, and the two have worked together since on many writing projects; Lane often appears as a character in Crozier's work. Many of Crozier's poems create strong female characters and voices; others have a strong political edge that cuts across areas far beyond the prairies or Canada. She has also been active as an anthologist of prairie writing, editing important collections like *A Sudden Radiance: Saskatchewan Poetry* (1987). Among her better-known books are *The Garden Going On without Us* (1985); *Inventing the Hawk* (1992), which won the Governor General's Award; *A Saving Grace: The Collected Poems of Mrs. Bentley* (1996), in which Crozier recreates the voice of Sinclair Ross's protagonist from his classic novel *As For Me and My House* (1941); *Apocrypha of Light* (2002); *Bones in Their Wings: Ghazals* (2003); and, most recently, *Whetstone* (2005). Crozier and Lane currently live in Victoria, where she teaches creative writing at the University of Victoria.

Introduction

Lorna Crozier's work enjoys a popularity among the general public that's rare for poetry in Canada. Valued for its "clarity and accessibility" (Hillis 15), it has been praised because, as Crozier puts it, "the ordinary person can read my work and understand it" (qtd. in Carey 16). Her books are also highly respected by her fellow poets, and have won numerous honours, including the Governor General's Award for *Inventing the Hawk*. Scholarly attention to her writing, especially in recent years, continues to grow. Critical approaches range from discussions of Crozier's deep connection to the landscape and culture of the Canadian prairies (e.g., Carey, Enright, Hillis, Keahey, Weis); to politicized analyses of her poetics of resistance to social injustices such as political violence (York) and sexual abuse (Boire); to complex theoretical readings of her mythological allusions as critiques of Western patriarchy (Gingell), her love poems as protests against female repression (MacDonald), and her use of the elegy as "parodic reinscription" of literary convention (Bowen 46). Clearly, Crozier has developed a voice with broad appeal, one that popular, literary, and academic readers can all appreciate.

The title of Crozier's "Poem about Nothing" could be read as a commentary on the aesthetic elements that have given her work such a wide and varied audience. As a meditation on the nature of zero, "Poem about Nothing" illustrates the strong elegiac impulse that runs throughout Crozier's work. The round numeral zero, "the one we didn't understand / at school," is a visual metaphor for loss or omission, and it's a fitting topic for a poet who desires to honour what is absent, whether in life or in literature. The poem exemplifies Crozier's style, in that its light, humorous tone and its elegant simplicity of language are deceptive, for "Poem about Nothing" resists its own title to blossom into a multi-layered engagement with a variety of substantial subjects until, ultimately, the poem is "about nothing" less than the central question of our existence: what is the relationship between being and not being? Like most of Crozier's work, "Poem about Nothing" explores profound philosophical, political, spiritual, and emotional issues, all the while appearing to be talking "about nothing" much. Crozier achieves this effect through an intense compression of language, a concentrated attention to allusion, imagery, line breaks, syntax, and diction. This dedication to poetic craft, combined with a radical imagination and a finely tuned emotional intelligence, produces work that is both accessible and sophisticated. With a kind of sleight of hand, Crozier fuses the ordinary and the extraordinary to reveal that our everyday lives, like the mundane numeral zero, are utterly mysterious and compelling. In the process, she performs an act that Clarise Foster has called "an unveiling of the miracle of the ordinary" (10).

The miraculous and the ordinary come together most creatively in Crozier's retellings of stories from the Bible. As Susan Gingell pointed out in 1991, "A constant re-visioning of Judeo-Christian myth has been a part of Crozier's work from the start" (75). In keeping with her thematic focus on absence, Crozier says she is especially interested in those elements that are missing from the stories of the Bible: "I have always wanted to turn what's been silent into language, whether it's been animal or female or the silence of lost places.... The Bible is a great minefield for this kind of translation" (qtd. in Foster 17–18). In the process, Crozier often inserts images of the "ordinary" Canadian prairies into the "extraordinary" stories of the Bible. In "Home Town," for example, she imagines Jesus Christ as a prairie boy: "He must have been from a town / with a Pool grain elevator, a Chinese cafe, / and one main street no one bothered to name." She also offers multiple interpretations of the stories she retells, a technique that not only expands the possibilities for understanding biblical tradition but also throws into question the whole notion of any single or official explanation for the order of things. Most significantly, however, her "translations" are part of a long and venerable tradition of feminist revisions to the Bible, paying homage to the female figures whose voices are so seldom heard in Scripture.

In "On the Seventh Day," Crozier revises the Creation story in Genesis 1, setting it on the Canadian prairie and using it to satirize the tradition of male dominance in the arts. Like some poetic genius of the Romantic era, Crozier's God is "the dreamy sort," forgetful and inept when it comes to practical matters. His wife is a traditional homemaker and helpmate, busy with "the many chores / a wife must do in the vast / though dustless rooms of heaven" or "visiting his mother." Crozier's subtle reference to God's mother marks him as one of the created, a creature born of a female. God, however, is caught up in his role as Creator: "God said / Let there be light. / And there was light." Apparently mesmerized by his ability to create light by mere proclamation, God repeats the procedure day after day, very nearly forgetting to create the earth at all. On the sixth day, his wife has to remind him urgently, *"Quick ... make something to stand on!"* As a result, the earth is an afterthought, nothing but a "thin spit of earth / under that huge prairie sky." This image offers an alternative explanation for the entry of death into the world. In Genesis, mortality is God's punishment for the disobedience of Adam and Eve (Genesis 3:19). In Crozier's account, death is the result of God's absent-minded self-absorption, for after he made all that light, "there was too little room / for life without end."

"On the Seventh Day" is delightfully humorous, with its reference to the prairie sky (a sly suggestion that the Garden of Eden might be found in Saskatchewan), and its parody of the egocentric, impractical patriarch, who must be rescued by his wife. Yet the poem also raises serious questions about the nature of power. On the seventh day, God's wife has work to do: "Everything he'd forgotten / she had to create." But God, the mighty poet, retires to his study where he inscribes the Genesis account, "changing all the facts, of course, / even creating Woman / from a Man's rib." God's wife dismisses his fantastical account: "Who's going to believe it?" But "the word," which has the power to create, also has the power to exclude. Because God has a room of his own, and the leisure time to write, his authority prevails, and the female role in Creation—literally, the work of *home-making*—is erased from the record.

"Original Sin" also looks at an element that has been erased from the Bible, drawing on the apocryphal myth of Lilith. According to ancient myth, Lilith was the first wife of Adam, a woman who viewed herself as his equal (see Meyers). But Lilith appears nowhere in the Bible. "Original Sin" suggests that Lilith's exclusion came about because of her closeness with Eve, a form of female solidarity that threatened patriarchal power in the Garden. The opening stanza describes the closeness of Lilith and Eve, their existence as "one creature." In an image reminiscent of a prairie country fair, where such anomalies of nature might be on exhibit, Lilith describes herself and Eve as "a calf so strange we would be kept / inside a jar." Apparently there is no place, and no word, for female intimacy in the Garden of Eden. Only a heretic like the astronomer Galileo, "with his telescope / and blasphemy" could have "named" the women's "double brightness," because the sisterhood of Lilith and Eve exists outside of the language, and the accepted norms, of the Garden. Lilith's "first argument with God" is her resistance to physical separation from Eve: "I didn't want to leave her. I clung to the womb / with my nails and teeth, ripped night from day, / eternity from now." Here, Lilith claims responsibility not only for the pain of childbirth but also for the partition of night from day and the divisive creation of time itself—accomplishments traditionally attributed to God (Genesis 1:14 and 3:16). Lilith also resists the sexual dominance of Adam, refusing to "lie placid" beneath him, and so she is exiled from Eden. The image of Lilith and Eve as one body, the association of Lilith with rebellion against authority, and Lilith's exclusion from Eden, combine to suggest that "Lilith" is the name for the rebellious desires of Eve, which have been tamed, or purged, by the God who "honed away everything she'd been." After Lilith's banishment, Eve can barely recall this lost aspect of her own nature: "I said *Lilith* / though I didn't remember / what it meant." Like Genesis, Crozier's "Original Sin" tells a story of transgression, punishment, and a tragic fall into a world suffused with longing. But while the Genesis story figures the punishment as a separation from God, "Original Sin" suggests that the punishment is the separation of women from each other and their subsequent fall from power.

One of the most harrowing stories of Genesis is that of the near sacrifice of Isaac by his father Abraham. In Genesis 22, God tests Abraham's loyalty by ordering him to take young Isaac up the side of a mountain and offer him as a sacrifice. Abraham complies, but before he can strike the fatal blow, an angel of the Lord comes down and tells him to sacrifice a ram instead. It is a story that has been retold many times, perhaps most subversively by Wilfred Owen in his anti-war poem "The Parable of the Old Man and the Young." Crozier, in "The Sacrifice of Isaac," invents a new and shocking twist. Isaac is saved, not by an angel of the Lord, but by Isaac's mother, absent in the original tale, who arises at the crucial moment to slit "the bare throat of [her] husband's / Lord." Crozier's final line break seems to merge the identities of Abraham and his Lord, implying that perhaps the human father invokes the power of God in order to tyrannize his family. "The Sacrifice of Isaac" protests such domestic violence with vivid, unmistakable fury. Like "On the Seventh Day" and "Original Sin," it revokes the agency of God and hands the power over to a woman. Although some readers might view these biblical revisions as blasphemous, others view them as a way of marrying the miraculous and the ordinary, reminders of the potential for transformative power in our everyday lives. Crozier's prairie images work to bring these stories "home," not only to prairie readers but to all of us, by suggesting that they might take place anywhere. And like the landscape, her biblical characters are oddly familiar. Her "God" is recognizable as that aspect of ourselves that is egocentric, caught up in the importance of our own desires, possessive of our own creations, and forgetful of the needs and experiences of others. Her "Lilith" is the name for that aspect of ourselves that is wild and vulnerable and buried; her "Eve" the name for our sense of loss; and Isaac's mother a sign of our outraged sense of justice. Crozier's interpretations don't reject Scripture, but open it up, inviting us to take part in the stories of the Bible, even as she takes those stories apart.

In *A Saving Grace*, Crozier takes on a canonical text of a very different kind: Sinclair Ross's novel *As for Me and My House* (1941). Ross's novel has been immensely influential in Canadian writing, particularly on the prairies, and in a 1985 interview, Crozier described its effect on her as an emerging writer:

> That's when my head flew open, when I read Sinclair Ross's *As for Me and My House*. I thought, Oh my God, he's writing about *my* landscape. That was really important to me, that he should write about the wind, the dust, the false-front stores. I think my education began then. It was the discovery of my own country. Somewhere in my mind I said, If these people can write and they are born here, maybe I can too. (qtd. in Hillis 6)

Ross's novel is a story of drought, poverty, and unrequited love, set in the fictional small town of Horizon in Depression-era Saskatchewan and narrated by the wife of the repressed Reverend Philip Bentley. Mrs. Bentley is a musician who has given up her artistic ambition in order to marry Philip. Yet she is consumed with guilt over her belief that Philip gave up his own ambitions as a visual artist in order to marry her. Mrs. Bentley can't quite see the contradiction, but Crozier's Mrs. Bentley has a clearer view of things. Crozier enriches the original text, both by weaving in the "numerous local histories" she lists in her book's acknowledgements (93) and by drawing out the novel's feminist subtext, which went unnoticed for decades after its publication.

Crozier revises Ross's prose, allowing Mrs. Bentley to express herself as a poet, an identity described as "this other thing / I keep from all of them" ("Not the Music"). The voice of the poems is convincing as the inner, lyrical voice of the original Mrs. Bentley, expressing a braver, more self-aware aspect of herself that's hinted at but never fully realized in Ross's novel. As many readers have noted, Mrs. Bentley's self-effacement is underlined by the absence of her first name from the novel. This omission becomes the topic of Crozier's poem "Mrs. Bentley," in which the narrator is well aware of her own namelessness and teases the reader by listing a number of possible names for herself: "Gladys, Louise, Madeline? / I fancy Margaret…." Here, Crozier refuses to read the absence of a first name as a sign of Mrs. Bentley's insignificant status in the novel as "a fungus or parasite whose life depends on [Philip]" (Ross 151). Instead, she playfully exploits the absence in order to liberate Mrs. Bentley from a fixed identity, placing her in control and allowing her to name herself as she pleases. Similarly, Crozier exploits Philip's failure to draw a portrait of his wife, in order to let her portray herself. Mrs. Bentley does so boldly, describing her own insightful "prairie eye" that sees "what lies just over / where the lines converge." She also speaks of erotic love with an openness that Ross's Mrs. Bentley never could, evoking "my flesh warmed by his hands, / the taste of me on his tongue" ("Mrs. Bentley"). Although this voice differs from the original, the insights and passions of Crozier's Mrs. Bentley are present, just below the surface, on almost every page of Ross's novel. Similarly, but in a more sombre vein, "The Kind of Woman" draws on the gothic horror of female dependency that lies at the heart of Ross's novel, though it's never expressed so directly. As Crozier's Mrs. Bentley responds with deep empathy and fear to the failed suicide attempt of Emma Humphreys, an event that does not occur in Ross's novel, she views Emma as "the kind of woman / like you, like me," drawing a clear parallel between Emma's despair and her own. *A Saving Grace* is both an expansion of, and a loving homage to, Ross's novel, and to read the two texts side by side is to witness an important movement in the development of the literary imagination on the prairies, as one writer reads another.

Crozier's revisions of the Bible and her reinterpretation of *As for Me and My House* focus on the gaps in those texts, following up the traces of untold stories beneath the surface. This fascination with what's missing runs also throughout her more personal lyrics, many of which are elegies. In poems such as "How to Stop Missing Your Friend Who Died," "Living Day by Day," "Canada Day Parade," "The Dark Ages of the Sea," "Going Back," "Watching My Lover," and "What You Remember Remains," Crozier presents daily life as a series of losses, whether caused by distance, accident, illness, aging, or death. Like "Poem about Nothing," which states that "In the beginning God made zero," these poems seem to acknowledge that loss is not opposite to life, but an integral, even a beautiful, part of it.

In "Canada Day Parade," the speaker turns her attendance at a parade into an anecdote to entertain her friends, but confesses, "I didn't mention my father / sitting beside me." She leaves her father out of her story partly because the story is intended to amuse, and the father, in declining health, is not an amusing topic. More importantly, his failure to appear in her story is a continuation of his perpetual failure to appear in her life. In her childhood, he was rarely beside her. Instead, he was "somewhere down the street, / alone and cocky, drunk or about to be" or "racing his speedboat / at Duncaren Dam, the waves / lifting him and banging him down." But these dynamic images are only memories. At the parade, the father is elderly and ill. The high-flying cocksure daredevil has been grounded, confined to a wheelchair, and the only thing airborne is "the smell of ammonia rising from his lap." The poem is an elegy to the younger, more vigorous father. In a sense, it is also an elegy to a father who never existed, a father who haunts the poem, though he is never mentioned, the one who would have been more present in his daughter's life.

The absent father also plays a small but significant role in "Mother and I, Walking," which describes a mother drawing her daughter inside her coat to protect her from the winter wind. The two females walk so closely together that their footprints in the snow look like "the tracks of one animal / crossing the open." This image, similar to that of the "four-legged" Lilith / Eve in "Original Sin," evokes the intimate bond between mother and daughter. But despite the poem's focus on this bond, its very first line is "Father is gone again," suggesting that his absence saturates the moment. In an autobiographical essay, Crozier recounts a similar event in a way that provides context for this poem, exploring the ambivalence of a daughter toward a beloved but unreliable father whose disappearances were among his most defining characteristics ("Breathing under Ice" 100).

In "A Kind of Love," the speaker realizes that her lover, like her father, is not fully present in her life, and she finds herself waiting, as her mother often waited, on his return. The relationship described is not the idealized romantic love of storybooks. But the speaker says it is "the kind / I'm most familiar with— / the weight I claim / I cannot bear and do, / and do." Crozier's careful line break isolates the phrase "the weight I claim," emphasizing that the speaker is owning this painful love, staking a claim to it. The desire for the absent lover is not a burden that she can simply throw off, nor does she want to. The final two lines echo Milton Acorn's poem "I've Tasted My Blood," with its protest against suffering and its angry prayer "that this won't be and be" and also Sylvia Plath's angry poem "Daddy," with its sardonic parody of the marriage vows: "And I said I do, I do." The repetition expresses the anger that accompanies this "kind of love" with an intense clarity. There is no simple dichotomy here, between "good" and "bad" relationships. The desire for the absent beloved is never cured, but remains what it is, a powerful, complicated, and compelling force. When read together, "Canada Day Parade," "Mother and I, Walking," and "A Kind of Love" illuminate each other, intensify each other's sense of longing, and raise the possibility that love itself is created by loss.

Crozier's elegiac impulse is present even in poems that don't announce themselves as elegies. "Quitting Smoking," for example, is a humorous piece, and thus a reader might be tempted to regard it as slight. But the critic Deborah Bowen has pointed out its use of classic elegiac elements. For example, Bowen notes that "the desire for the beloved (the cigarette) is projected onto everything in the external environment" (51). Similarly, in "Wildflowers," Crozier comments on "the heart's strange fondness / for what is lost." In "The Red Onion in Skagway, Alaska," she notes, "The only thing this town's / got going is the past." In "The Wild Boys," the young girl is most attracted to the boys' wounds and missing teeth, those "parts they left behind or / lost." And in "The Goldberg Variations," the music seems sweeter because Glenn Gould, who died in 1982, is playing it "his last time."

Crozier's finest works could be said to be poems about nothing. Her explorations into the nature of absence reveal that the gaps in our stories leave room for imaginative revision, the gaps in our lives are sites of intense desire, and loss itself has its own peculiar beauty. As Leonard Cohen says, in a song Crozier quotes as epigraph to *Everything Arrives at the Light*, "There is a crack in everything. / That's how the light gets in." The poems collected here represent only a fraction of Lorna Crozier's work. It is hoped that the reader of this volume will enjoy them and then, like Crozier, become suspicious about what's missing, begin to desire it, and seek out the poems that are absent here.

—*Catherine Hunter*

Works Cited

Acorn, Milton. "I've Tasted My Blood." *The New Oxford Book of Canadian Verse in English*. Ed. Margaret Atwood. Toronto: Oxford, 1982. 236.

Boire, Gary. "Transparencies: Of Sexual Abuse, Ambivalence, and Resistance." *Essays on Canadian Writing* 51/52 (Winter 1993/Spring 1994): 211–32.

Bowen, Deborah. "Phoenix from the Ashes: Lorna Crozier and Margaret Avison in Contemporary Mourning." *Canadian Poetry: Studies, Documents, Reviews* 40 (Spring / Summer 1997): 46–57.

Carey, Barbara. "Against the Grain." *Books in Canada* 22. 3 (April 1993): 14–17.

Cohen, Leonard. "Anthem." *The Future*. Columbia, 53226, 1992.

Crozier, Lorna. *Angels of Flesh, Angels of Silence*. Toronto: McClelland and Stewart, 1988.

——. *Apocrypha of Light*. Toronto: McClelland and Stewart, 2002.

——. "Breathing under Ice." *Addicted: Notes from the Belly of the Beast*. Ed. Lorna Crozier and Patrick Lane. Vancouver: Douglas and McIntyre, 2001. 85–103.

——. *Everything Arrives at the Light*. Toronto: McClelland and Stewart, 1995.

——. *The Garden Going On without Us*. Toronto: McClelland and Stewart, 1985.

——. *Humans and Other Beasts*. Winnipeg: Turnstone, 1980.

——. *Inventing the Hawk*. Toronto: McClelland and Stewart, 1992.

——. *A Saving Grace*. Toronto: McClelland and Stewart, 1996.

——. *What the Living Won't Let Go*. Toronto: McClelland and Stewart, 1999.

Enright, Robert. "Literary Landscaping: A Symposium on Prairie Landscape Memory and Literary Tradition." *Border Crossings* 6.4 (Fall 1987): 32–38.

Foster, Clarise. "An Interview with Lorna Crozier." *Contemporary Verse 2* 25.3 (Winter 2003): 9–19.

Gingell, Susan. "Let Us Revise Mythologies: The Poetry of Lorna Crozier." *Essays on Canadian Writing* 43 (Spring 1991): 67–82.

Hillis, Doris. "The Real Truth, the *Poetic Truth*." *Prairie Fire* 6.3 (Summer 1985): 4–15.

Keahey, Deborah. *Making It Home: Place in Canadian Prairie Literature*. Winnipeg: U of Manitoba P, 1998.

MacDonald, Tanis. "Regarding the Male Body: Rhapsodic Contradiction in Lorna Crozier's 'Penis Poems.'" *English Studies in Canada* 28.2 (June 2002): 247–67.

Meyers, Carol, gen. ed. *Women in Scripture: A Dictionary of Named and Unnamed Women in the Hebrew Bible, the Apocryphal/Deuterocanonical Books, and the New Testament*. Grand Rapids, MI: William B. Eerdmans, 2000.

Owen, Wilfred. "The Parable of the Old Man and the Young." *Wilfred Owen: War Poems and Others*. Ed. Dominic Hibberd. London: Chatto and Windus, 1973.

Plath, Sylvia. "Daddy." *Ariel*. 1965. Perennial Classics Edition. New York: Harper-Collins, 1999. 56–59.

Ross, Sinclair. *As for Me and My House*. 1941. New Canadian Library Edition. Toronto: McClelland and Stewart, 1970.

Weis, Lyle. "Lorna Uher: 'A Poet to Be Grateful For'—Margaret Laurence." *Essays on Canadian Writing* 18/19 (1980): 179–82.

York, Lorraine M. "Home Thoughts or Abroad? A Rhetoric of Place in Modern and Postmodern Canadian Political Poetry." *Essays on Canadian Writing* 51/52 (Winter 1993/Spring 1994): 321–39.

Still-Life

When you are drunk with rage and fear
lower the glass bell over time

think of the stilled, the frozen
moment: the final second before the bird's

pristine flight from the breathless
lake, the bee caught in the clear jar

the cat's stiff body that melts
to bone under the steady sun

Those quiet moments when you don't know
I am looking: your hand poised above

the page before the first word or the last
the pause of the match held to your cigarette

as you lie naked after loving. When you are
mad with guilt, and throw it like knives

pinning the hour-glass curve to the wall
hold these still-lifes in your hands

intervals of silence before you come
and the held breath breaks

Poem about Nothing

Zero is the one we didn't understand
at school. Multiplied by anything
it remains nothing.

When I ask my friend
the mathematician who studies rhetoric
if zero is a number, he says *yes*
and I feel great relief.

If it were a landscape
it would be a desert.
If it had anything to do
with anatomy, it would be
a mouth, a missing limb,
a lost organ.

    Ø

Zero worms its way
                between one and one
and changes everything.
It slips inside the alphabet.
It is the vowel on a mute tongue,
the pupil in a blind man's eye,
the image
       of the face
he holds on his fingertips.

    Ø

When you look up
from the bottom of a dry well
zero is what you see,
the terrible blue of it.

It is the rope
you knot around your throat
when your heels itch for wings.

Icarus understood zero
as he caught the smell
of burning feathers
and fell into the sea.

Ø

If you roll zero down a hill
it will grow,
swallow the towns, the farms,
the people at their tables
playing tic-tac-toe.

Ø

When the Cree chiefs
signed the treaties on the plains
they wrote *X*
beside their names.

In English, X equals zero.

Ø

I ask my friend
the rhetorician who studies mathematics
What does zero mean and keep it simple.

He says *Zip.*

Ø

Zero is the pornographer's number.
He orders it through the mail
under a false name. It is the number
of the last man on death row,

the number of the girl who jumps
three stories to abort.

Zero starts and ends
at the same place. Some compare it
to driving across the Prairies all day
and feeling you've gone nowhere.

    Ø   Ø   Ø

In the beginning God made zero.

This Is a Love Poem without Restraint

This poem
is full of pain
full of pieces
It cries out
oh! oh! oh!
It has no pride
no discretion
It whimpers
It will not drop its eyes
when it meets a stranger
It will not hide
its tears

•

It will talk
of beauty
Lilacs Apples
The smell of rain
in caraganas
Your mouth
your eyes

What are you going to do about it?
You cannot stop me
now

•

The moon shines on this page
as the poem writes
itself. It is trying to find
whiteness
frost on snow
two feathers

on a pillow
your hands
          upon
my skin

    ●

These words are tired
of being
          words
They refuse to sit here
pretending
          they can't move
                              off the page

These are the first
ones to leave
their white space
They fall
on your tongue
letter
          by
              letter
like raindrops

One of them
is my name

What will you do with it?
It has decided to live
inside you

    ●

This poem has no restraint
It will not say
plum blossom
sunset

rubbing stone
cat's cradle

It refuses to be evasive

I miss you
I miss you
Come home

•

It won't talk of passion
but the sleep that follows
when our bodies
touch

that moment
just before waking
when we realize
we've been holding one another
in our sleep

•

How do you use the word *love*
in a poem?

Love.

If you look at it
long enough
it will burn into your eyes

The Child Who Walks Backwards

My next-door neighbour tells me
her child runs into things.
Cupboard corners and doorknobs
have pounded their shapes
into his face. She says
he is bothered by dreams,
rises in sleep from his bed
to steal through the halls
and plummet like a wounded bird
down the flight of stairs.

This child who climbed my maple
with the sureness of a cat,
trips in his room, cracks
his skull on the bedpost,
smacks his cheeks on the floor.
When I ask about the burns
on the back of his knee,
his mother tells me
he walks backwards
into fireplace grates
or sits and stares at flames
while sparks burn stars in his skin.

Other children write their names
on the casts that hold
his small bones.
His mother tells me
he runs into things,
walks backwards,
breaks his leg
while she lies
sleeping.

Carrots

Carrots are fucking
the earth. A permanent
erection, they push deeper
into the damp and dark.
All summer long
they try so hard to please.
Was it good for you,
was it good?

Perhaps because the earth won't answer
they keep on trying.
While you stroll through the garden
thinking *carrot cake,*
carrots and onions in beef stew,
carrot pudding with caramel sauce,
they are fucking their brains out
in the hottest part of the afternoon.

Onions

The onion loves the onion.
It hugs its many layers,
saying O, O, O,
each vowel smaller
than the last.

Some say it has no heart.
It doesn't need one.
It surrounds itself,
feels whole. Primordial.
First among vegetables.

If Eve had bitten it
instead of the apple,
how different
Paradise.

Fear of Snakes

The snake can separate itself
from its shadow, move on ribbons of light,
taste the air, the morning and the evening,
the darkness at the heart of things. I remember
when my fear of snakes left for good,
it fell behind me like an old skin. In Swift Current
the boys found a huge snake and chased me
down the alleys, Larry Moen carrying it like a green torch,
the others yelling, *Drop it down her back*, my terror
of its sliding in the runnel of my spine (Larry,
the one who touched the inside of my legs on the swing,
an older boy we knew we shouldn't get close to
with our little dresses, our soft skin), my brother
saying *Let her go*, and I crouched behind the caraganas,
watched Larry nail the snake to a telephone pole.
It twisted on twin points of light, unable to crawl
out of its pain, its mouth opening, the red
tongue tasting its own terror, I loved it then,
that snake. The boys standing there with their stupid hands
dangling from their wrists, the beautiful green
mouth opening, a terrible dark O
no one could hear.

Quitting Smoking

The phone says smoke when it rings, the radio says smoke, the TV smokes its own images until they are dead butts at three A.M. Three A.M. and the *dépanneurs* are open just for you. White cartons, blue cartons, silver cartons that mirror your face. Behind the counters, the young men who work the night-shift unwrap the cellophane as lovingly as you undo the buttons of a silk shirt, your fingers burning.

•

Your cat is grey. When he comes in from the muddy lane, his paws leave ashes on the floor. The dirty burner on the stove smokes, the kettle smokes, your first, your last cup of coffee demands a smoke. The snow on the step is a long Vogue paper waiting to be rolled. Above the chimneys stars light up and smoke the whole night through.

•

In Montreal there are stores where you can buy one cigarette. Cars parked outside, idle, exhaust pipes smoking. Women you could fall in love with approach you from the shadows and offer a light. The sound of a match struck on the black ribbon of a matchbox is the sound of a new beginning. In every dark room across the city, the fireflies of cigarettes are dancing, their small bodies burning out.

•

Dawn and the neon cross on the mountain melts in the pale light. Another day. Blindfolded and one last wish. Electric, your fingers ignite everything they touch—the curtains, the rug, the sleeping cat. The air around your body crackles and sparks, your hair a halo of fire.

•

Breathe in, breathe out. Your lungs are animals pacing their cages of bone, eyes burning holes through your chest. The shape of your mouth around an imaginary cigarette is an absence you can taste. Your lips acetylene, desire begins and ends on the tip of your tongue.

•

The grey of morning—smoke from the sun settling on the roofs, the snow, the bare branches of maple trees. Every cell in your body is a mouth, crying to be heard: *O Black Cat; O ageless Sailor, where have you gone? O Craven A, first letter of the alphabet, so beautiful to say, O Cameo…*

The Goldberg Variations

Never have I felt so unconnected
to everything. Light and its absence.
Rain. The cat on the windowsill catching flies.
Glenn Gould playing the Goldberg Variations
his last time.
           The endless variations of you,
making coffee, ordering seeds for the garden,
calling me upstairs to love. By our bed,
in *Equinox* a photo of an astronaut,
solitary figure
                floating in the cold blue
of space, connected to nothing, touching
nothing. Gould's fingers on ivory keys.
It isn't Bach he's playing
from the grave, the stopped heart.
So free of gravity the mind lifts
like a feathered seed, only
a thin shell of bone holding it in.
Not Bach, but music before it became
the least bit human.
           Is this ecstasy,
this strange remoteness? Rain falling
from such a distance. Gould's Goldberg
Variations. Your hands. The cold
cold blue. My skin.

Home Town

I like the kid who wrote on his first year
history paper: "The Holy land is sorta like
Christ's Home Town."

He must have been from a town
with a Pool grain elevator, a Chinese cafe,
and one main street no one bothered to name.
One of those places you leave
but want to come back to.
A place where your friends return
for the high school reunion (there were only six
in your graduating class), where you fall in love again
with your grade nine sweetheart and marry her
and it works.

One of those places you dream about
when you're stuck in the city on a muggy day
and the desert you have to cross to get there
keeps growing.

Not that it's perfect,
not that it doesn't have its share of wife-beating,
racism and down-right human greed.
But Christ would've liked the town
this kid's from. Maybe it's even got a name
like *Manyberries, Porcupine Plain,* or *Paradise Hill.*

Male Thrust

I can take no pleasure from serious reading ... that lacks a strong male thrust.
　　　　　　　　　　　　　　　　　　—Anthony Burgess

　　This poem bends its knees
　　and moves its groin.
　　It does the Dirty Dog
　　at parties. It pushes
　　against cloth, against
　　the page. It pokes
　　between the lines.
　　It breathes deeply,
　　closes its one eye
　　and wets its lips.
　　It writes lewd words
　　in the margins.
　　Wherever you are reading—
　　on a bus, at home
　　in your favourite chair,
　　in the library—
　　it flips open its coat
　　and flashes.
　　It backs the librarian
　　against the wall,
　　it comes
　　all over the stacks,
　　over *A Clockwork Orange*,
　　over *The Naked and the Dead*,
　　over *A Golden Treasury of Verse*,
　　over *Sexus*, *Nexus* and *Plexus*.
　　This poem won't stop.
　　Even when you close the book
　　you can hear it
　　making obscene sounds,
　　smacking its lips,
　　completely in love
　　with itself.

Mother and I, Walking

Father is gone again,
the streets empty.
Everyone is inside,
listening to radios
in the warm glow of their stoves.

The cold cries under our boots.
We wade through wind. It pushes
snow under my scarf and collar,
up the sleeves of my jacket.

Mother opens her old muskrat coat,
pulls me inside.
Her scent wraps around me.
The back of my head presses
into the warm rise of her belly.

When I lower my eyes, I see
our feet, mine between hers,
the tracks of one animal
crossing the open,
strange and nocturnal,
moving towards home.

How to Stop Missing Your Friend Who Died

The moon over Vancouver Harbour
is full and red.
Through the window
you can see a barge go by.
It is empty, returning
to whatever country sent it out.

You can't see any lights
but someone must be steering,
someone who doesn't know
you are sitting behind a window
that overlooks the sea.
The moonlight makes the barge
more important than it really is.

Then there's a sailboat
and a heron.
Its legs stretch so far behind
when it's flying
it forgets they're there.

On the Seventh Day

On the first day God said
Let there be light.
And there was light.
On the second day
God said, *Let there be light,*
and there was more light.

What are you doing? asked God's wife,
knowing he was the dreamy sort.
You created light yesterday.

I forgot, God said. *What can I do
about it now?*

Nothing, said his wife.
But pay attention!
And in a huff she left
to do the many chores
a wife must do in the vast
though dustless rooms of heaven.

On the third day God said
Let there be light. And
on the fourth and fifth
(his wife off visiting his mother).

When she returned there was only
the sixth day left. The light
was so blinding, so dazzling
God had to stretch and stretch the sky to hold it
and the sky took up all the room—
it was bigger than anything
even God could imagine.
Quick, his wife said,

make something to stand on!
God cried, *Let there be earth!*
and a thin line of soil
nudged against the sky like a run-over snake
bearing all the blue in the world on its back.

On the seventh day God rested
as he always did. Well, *rest*
wasn't exactly the right word,
his wife had to admit.
On the seventh day God
went into his study
and wrote in his journal
in huge curlicues and loops
and large crosses on the *t*'s,
changing all the facts, of course,
even creating Woman
from a Man's rib, imagine that!
But why be upset? she thought.
Who's going to believe it?

Anyway, she had her work to do.
Everything he'd forgotten
she had to create
with only a day left to do it.
Leaf by leaf,
paw by paw, two by two,
and now nothing
could be immortal
as in the original plan.

Go out and multiply, yes,
she'd have to say it,
but there was too little room
for life without end,
forever and ever,
on that thin spit of earth
under that huge prairie sky.

Living Day by Day

I have no children and he has five,
three of them grown up, two with their mother.
It didn't matter when I was thirty and we met.
There'll be no children, he said, the first night
we slept together and I didn't care,
thought we wouldn't last anyway,
those terrible fights,
he and I struggling to be the first
to pack, the first one out the door.
Once I made it to the car before him,
locked him out. He jumped on the hood,
then kicked the headlights in.
Our friends said we'd kill each other
before the year was through.

Now it's ten years later.
Neither of us wants to leave.
We are at home with one another,
we are each other's home,
the voice in the doorway,
calling *Come in, come in,*
it's growing dark.

Still, I'm often asked if I have children.

Sometimes I answer yes.
Sometimes we have so much
we make another person.
I can feel her in the night
slip between us, tell my dreams
how she spent her day. *Good night,*
she says, *good night, little mother,*
and leaves before I waken.
Across the lawns she dances
in her white, white dress,
her dream hair flying.

Angel of Bees

The honeycomb
that is the mind
storing things

crammed with sweetness,
eggs about to hatch—
the slow thoughts

growing wings and legs,
humming memory's
five seasons, dancing

in the brain's blue light,
each turn and tumble
full of consequence,

distance and desire.
Dangerous to disturb
this hive, inventing clover.

How the mind wants
to be free of you,
move with the swarm,

ascend in the shape
of a blossoming tree—
your head on the pillow

emptied of scent and colour,
winter's cold indifference
moving in.

Canada Day Parade

Two days later and I've turned the parade
into a story I tell over drinks. Start with
my favourite part, the band from Cabri,
the whole town marching, children
barely bigger than their horns,
old men and women keeping time. Then,
riding bareback, four Lions' Ladies
in fake leather fringes,
faces streaked with warpaint, not one
real Indian in the whole parade.
Finally the Oilman's Float, a long
flatbed truck with a pumping machine,
a boy holding a sign saying "Future Oilman,"
beside him a girl, the "Future Oilman's wife."
I tell my friends it was as if I'd stumbled
into a movie set in the fifties, that simple
stupid time when everyone was so unaware.

That's my story about the parade,
three parts to the narrative,
a cast of characters, a summing up.
I didn't mention my father
sitting beside me in a wheel chair.
Out of hospital for the day.
My mother putting him in diapers.
In the fifties he wouldn't have been
here beside us but somewhere down the street,
alone and cocky, drunk or about to be.
Or he'd have been racing his speedboat
at Duncaren Dam, the waves
lifting him and banging him down,
a violence he could understand,
that same dumb force raging inside him.

I don't describe my father
in his winter jacket, his legs covered
with a blanket in the hot light
bouncing off the pavement,
the smell of ammonia rising from his lap.

The day after the parade mom called
to say she saw us on TV.
When the camera panned the street
it stopped at us. "Not your dad," she said,
"they just caught the corner of his blanket."
As if he wasn't there.
As if he'd disappeared,
his boat flying through the air,
the engine stalled,
the blades of his propeller
stopped.

The Dark Ages of the Sea

Because we are mostly
made of water and water
calls to water
like the ocean to the river,
the river to the stream,
there was a time when
children fell into wells.

It was a time of farms
across the grasslands,
ancient lakes
that lay beneath them,
and a faith in things
invisible, be it water
never seen or something
trembling in the air.

We are born to fall
and children fell,
some surviving
to tell the tale,
pulled from the well's
dark throat,
wet and blind with terror
like a calf
torn from the womb
with ropes.

Others diminished into ghosts,
rode the bucket up
and when you drank
became the cold shimmer
in your cup, the metallic
undertaste of nails

some boy had carried
in his pocket
or the silver locket
that held a small girl's
dreams.

In those days people
spoke to horses,
voices soft as bearded
wheat; music lived
inside a stone. Not to say
it was good, that falling,
but who could stop it?

We are made
of mostly water
and water calls to water
through centuries of reason
children fall
light and slender
as the rain.

The Red Onion in Skagway, Alaska

The only thing this town's
got going is the past.
Here the erotics of history,
and vice versa, bring prosperity.
In the Red Onion Saloon
I read what's supposed to be
an amusing tale of the girls upstairs
who worked in "cribs," ten by ten cells,
just enough room to lie
spread-legged. For efficiency

someone built a row of wooden dolls
behind the bar, an iron rod
through their ribs
joining them like paper cut-outs,
below each one
the number of a room.
When one of the girls was occupied
the bartender flipped a doll
onto her back
and when he righted her
another miner climbed the stairs.

The "Red-Rock Ladies" they were called
and on the wall a turn-of-the-century
photograph. Four small-town girls
open-faced and plump
look out at you
like someone in an ad for milk
or someone you used to know,
that quiet girl who caught the bus to school
from Olds or Antelope or Manyberries,
the one who ate her lunch outside alone.

They're in their Sunday best,
long skirts, high collars, all
the buttons buttoned up.
One holds a small dog,
another, a spotted cat.

I think of the ponies
who never got to leave the mines,
some born blind inside,
the stories go,
pulling car after car
in numbing dark. The photographer
has made the Red-Rock Ladies smile (I hope
his words were kind)

but they all look pale,
discomforted,
two with their reluctant pets
tucked into the fleshy curve of their arms,
in the Red Onion
perhaps all they knew
of love.

The Wild Boys

It was the wild ones you loved best,
the boys who sat surly at the front
where every teacher moved them,
the ones who finished midterms
first, who showed up late,
then never showed at all.

Under the glare of outdoor lights
you watched them bang
their hard bodies against the boards,
gloves and sticks flying.
In the cold they looked back at you
through stitched and swollen eyes,
smiled crookedly to hide
their missing teeth,
breathed through noses broken
in a game or pool-hall fight.
There was always someone older,
a fist and grin
they just couldn't walk away from,
there was always some girl, watching.

They were the first boys you knew
who owned a car, who rolled
a thin white paper, who talked
out of the side of their mouths,
cigarettes burning.
You watched them fall
quick and bright and beautiful
off the highest diving boards,
you watched them disappear
then throw themselves on top of you
till you thought you'd drown.

Oh, they were cool and mean,
but sometimes they treated you
with such extravagant tenderness,
giving you a rhinestone broach
they'd nicked from Woolworth's,
a fuzzy pink angora, giving up
their jackets on an autumn night
to keep you warm. How you loved
to move inside the shape of them,
the smell of sweat and leather
kissing your skin. For months
you wore their hockey rings
wound with gauze and tape
as if one day
you'd need to bind a wound.

The wild boys had the fastest
tongues, the dirtiest jokes,
and told anyone who'd listen
what they'd done to a girl
the night before
though in the narrow darkness
of a car or on a blanket
by the dam where eels slid
just beneath the surface, you knew
you did it to each other
and the words they said were sweet.

The boys you loved
knew everything, guided your mouth
and hands, showed you what you really
wanted from this life. Now,
it is their brokenness
you long to touch, the parts
they left behind or lost

as they learned too soon
too many years ago
what it took and took
to be a man.

The Garden at Night

Under the earth
radishes are the first
to light their lanterns,
spreading a watery glow
throughout the garden.

The star-nosed mole
who tunnels through the dark
thinks he is the chosen one,
all his paths suddenly
diffused with light.

Potatoes build their constellations
row on row like a child
trying to understand
the solar system,
each planet connected
by a string. Above,
tomatoes draw
what little warmth there is
inside, wax round
and glossy on their stems.

Digging to the surface
for the first time
the mole thinks he's found
another world—a sky
of moons, green and red,
each one growing larger
in his dark myopic eyes,
eclipsing all he knows
of earth.

Going Back

I stand across from the man I haven't seen
in fifteen years. He is my husband.
I look him in the eye.
I touch his thin brown fingers.
It is now fifteen years ago.
The dog we raised from a pup
turns in a circle on the doorstep.
She has dug her way out of the earth
as she used to dig in,
tunnelling after gophers.
There is dirt in her mouth and eyes.
She shakes her beautiful ears
and the flies that laid eggs in her skull
lift from her head, drift to the apples
unripening, turning back
into blossoms on the boughs.
I am about to speak.
The letter I wrote on the shore of Lake Winnipeg
when I ran away from him
returns to that place, unopened,
ink flowing backward into my pen.
The car coasts in reverse
down the gravel lane to our house.
I retrace my steps across the grass,
toe to heel   toe to heel
in slow motion over and over
rehearse the words
I never said fifteen years before.
He waits for me to speak, the door half open.
On the step, her collar too big,
the dog dreams back to her first rabbit,
her legs running and running
in that other world.

Dust

Rags stuffed under the doors,
around the windows
as if they were wounds
that needed staunching

yet the dust
settles everywhere,
on my skin, my hair, inside
my sleeves and collar.
I feel old, used up,
something found
in the back of a cupboard.

I cover the water crock
with a tea towel
embroidered with a *B*,
turn the dinner plates
face down on the table.
When we lift them
two moons glow
on the gritty cloth
and in the mornings when we rise,
the shape of our heads
remains on the pillowslips
as if we leave behind
the part of us
that keeps on dreaming.

The Kind of Woman

Yesterday they found Emma Humphreys
at the bottom of the dry well
on the neighbour's farm. Mrs. Bird
says there's no way she could have
fallen in. It was deliberate.
She threw herself and the baby
into the darkness and lay there
for three days until Rusty Howes
lowered a lantern on a rope
to take a look inside.
Just a hunch, he said.

When he saw her there,
the baby still and white as wax,
he didn't know if the kindest thing
was to walk away. But his brothers
eased him down, hand over hand,
to bring her up, still alive,
saying nothing, a dead
look in her eyes.
Her husband took her home.

He seems a decent man
but what goes on in houses
when no one's there
but family? A man,
a baby and his wife.

Dr. Bird said it was amazing
nothing was broken.

The church women at Mrs. Finley's
over tea wondered what kind of woman
would do a thing like that?

I wish I'd said the kind of woman
like you, like me

but I changed the subject
to next Sunday's hymns, afraid
if I talked of her, the darkness
she found more comforting than light,
I'd say too much. Who knows
what makes a woman leap
into a well with her baby,
lie there for three days—
that small death in her arms—

and not call out,
not call out,
for her own good reason
not wanting to be found.

Not the Music

Not the music.
It is this other thing
I keep from all of them
that matters, inviolable.

I scratch in my journals,
a mouse rummaging through cupboards,
nibbling on a crust of bread, apple skins,
chewing the edges of photographs, the small
details of a life. I hoard and save,
place one thing inside another
inside the next.

Start with the prairie, then Horizon
and inside it our house,
the kitchen, the table where I sit
with my journal, and inside it
everything I write—dust, moths,
wind speaking in whispers
across the page,
the absence of rain,
forgiveness—
everything shrinking
to the smallest
thinnest letter,
I.

Mrs. Bentley

I've walked through this story
in housedresses and splay-
footed rubbers. Mousy hair
without curls. Philip never drew
a convenient portrait
for me to comment on,
a hasty sketch. I could have said,
though his hand is flawless,
this does not resemble me.
That's my high forehead
and the way I purse my lips
but he's placed my eyes
far apart. I look in two directions.
The right one stares at you,
follows you as you move.
The left, my prairie eye,
gazes at what lies just over
where the lines converge.
No portraits exist, no photographs
and little self-description.
And nowhere in these pages
can you find my name.
Gladys, Louise, Madeline?
I fancy Margaret though in the country
everyone would call her Peg.
We're left with Mrs.
Bentley, dowdy, frumpy, plain.
Don't you wonder what Philip
called me as we lay together,
my flesh warmed by his hands,
the taste of me on his tongue,
as if there were no better sound
in all the world,
my name, my name!

Packing for the Future: Instructions

Take the thickest socks.
Wherever you're going
you'll have to walk.

There may be water.
There may be stones.
There may be high places
you cannot go without
the hope socks bring you,
the way they hold you
to the earth.

At least one pair must be new,
must be blue as a wish
hand-knit by your mother
in her sleep.

*

Take a leather satchel,
a velvet bag and an old tin box—
a salamander painted on the lid.

This is to carry that small thing
you cannot leave. Perhaps the key
you've kept though it doesn't fit
any lock you know,
the photograph that keeps you sane,
a ball of string to lead you out
though you can't walk back
into that light.

In your bag leave room for sadness,
leave room for another language.

There may be doors nailed shut.
There may be painted windows.
There may be signs that warn you
to be gone. Take the dream
you've been having since
you were a child, the one
with open fields and the wind
sounding.

    *

Mistrust no one who offers you
water from a well, a songbird's feather,
something that's been mended twice.
Always travel lighter
than the heart.

Watching My Lover

I watch him hold his mother
as she vomits into a bowl.
After, he washes her face
with a wet cloth and we try
to remove her soiled gown
tied in the back with strings.

Unable to lift her
I pull the green cotton
from under the blankets, afraid
I'll tear her skin.
He removes the paper diaper.
No one has taught us
how to do this, what to say.
Everything's so fragile here
a breath could break you.

She covers her breasts with hands
bruised from tubes and needles,
turns her face away.
It's okay, Mom, he says.
*Don't feel shy. I've undressed
dozens of women in my time.*
In this room where my lover
bares his mother, we three laugh.

Later, I curl naked beside him
in our bed, listen to his sleeping,
breath by breath. So worn out
he burns with fever—the fires
his flesh lights to keep him
from the cold.

Though he has washed
I smell her on his skin
as if she has licked him
from head to toe
with her old woman's tongue
so everyone who lies with him
will know he's still
his mother's son.

What You Remember Remains

The cockatoo named Joey wears
my father's hooded eyes, his look
of dumb surprise at dying. *Kiss me*,
Joey says, which isn't what he means.
It's cockatoo for *feed me* or, better yet,
my father small and turning yellow
in his bed, cockatoo for *set me free*.

Our new cat glides through the door
on your mother's legs, long and white.
In a wicker basket on my desk
she crosses her slim ankles
and seems as vain, your mother
hitching up her skirt when she thought
no one could see, the lace of her slip
lisping above her knees.

Yesterday a crow strode across the grass
with my Welsh Grandpa's stiffness
as if the bird had ruined his knees
from sixty years of gardening. Now
I put out jam on scraps of bread
and bother him with roses,
ask why the buds won't open,
how much bone they need to grow.

Kiss me—at least we know
what it means and who is speaking.
Sometimes late at night they come to us
with what they carry from the past,
that look, that way of walking,
that softness around the mouth
where grief begins.

A Kind of Love

You can see it
in my graduation photograph.
You're Daddy's little girl, he said,
his arm heavy around my shoulders,
his face too naked, a sloppy
smile sliding to one side.
I held him up. Mom tied his shoes.
His love made me ashamed.

Some days I felt protective,
his hangdog look at breakfast
when no one talked to him but me,
sugar spilling from his spoon.
Don't tell Mum, he'd say
on Sundays when he took me boating,
sunk his third empty in the lake.
At home, she fried a chicken
in case he didn't catch a fish,
waited and kept things warm.
Even so, he died too soon.

Now I wait for you as if
you've spent a summer afternoon
in waves of wind and sunlight. I know
you've hidden a bottle somewhere
upstairs in your room. So far
I've stopped myself from looking
though I can't find what to do.

More and more I'm Daddy's
little girl in peau de soi,
my first long dress, its false
sheen a wash of mauve.

When you lean into me
the same look's on your face
as in the photograph,
your smile's undone.

Among the other things
it could be named
this too is love, the kind
I'm most familiar with—
the weight I claim
I cannot bear and do,
and do.

Wildflowers

Wild Western Bergamot, Larkspur,
Closed Gentian near the Manitoba border,
Windflowers in the Cypress Hills.
I read the names out loud,
flip page after page as if the past were
a botanist with whom I've made a pact.
Evening Primrose, Yarrow, Wild Flax—
what would Sorrow look like, what fruit
would it bear? I have in mind no colour.
Yellow, red, or blue it would bloom
in rich abundance this July, its flowers
a burden, a fragrant heaviness,
between my fingers its leaves softly
furred, the fine hairs of a lover's wrist.
If I touched the sepals with my tongue
I'd say *anise* and then repeat it, an aftertaste,
a hint of time. Wild near the marsh
I find a kind of Rue where only yesterday
leopard-spotted frogs leapt in imitation
of the heart's strange fondness
for what is lost.

The Origin of the Species

... but the old man said that it was pointless to speak of there being no horses in the world for God would not permit such a thing.
— Cormac McCarthy, *All the Pretty Horses*

Drenched with dawn
eohippus, smaller than a fox,
walked out of chaos.

She struck the sand. Water
gushed from her hoofprint,
drops flying through the air

and where they fell
the sky came down to rest
and a thousand miracles of grass

meadowed the desert.
For centuries eohippus lived
satisfied and self-contained

then her legs and muzzle lengthened,
muscles pushed against
her withers, thickened her neck.

Now, ready for the wind
she made it lean and boneless,
its mane and tail visible
across the sky. Imagine
horse and wind
in the sun's warm pastures

before the fall. Imagine
the two of them alone
adrift in the absolute

beatitude of grass,
no insect biting,
no rope or bridle.

In the mornings of that lost
and long ago beginning,
nothing broken

or in need of breaking.

What the Snake Brings to the World

Without the snake
there'd be no letter *S*.
No forked tongue and toil,
no pain and sin. No wonder
the snake's without shoulders.
What could bear such a weight!

The snake's responsible for everything
that slides and hisses, that moves
without feet or legs. The wind, for example.
The sea in its long sweeps to shore and out again.

The snake has done some good, then.
Even sin to the ordinary man
brings its pleasures. And without
the letter *S* traced belly-wise
outside the gates of Eden
we'd have to live
with the singular of everything:
sparrow, ear, heartbeat,
mercy, truth.

Original Sin

1. The First Woman

We were mothers giving birth
to each other, or we were sisters,
our home the night's vast womb.
We orbited inside its silky
black cocoon. If Galileo had been
there with his telescope
and blasphemy, he would have named
our double brightness
and I wouldn't have been so lost.

My hand reached out
and to prove I was the first
the angels tied it with a strong red string,
the origin of scarlet as a curse.
I felt her grow beside me, her spirit curve
against my bones like cream inside a spoon.

We were one creature then,
four-legged, perhaps a fawn
whose hooves had not grown hard,
a calf so strange we would be kept
inside a jar. Then I counted fingers,
counted toes, and she looked back at me.

I, not Eve, brought pain into the birthing room.
I didn't want to leave her. I clung to the womb
with my nails and teeth, ripped night from day,
eternity from now.

That was my first argument with God.
The second: I wouldn't lie placid

as a hooked and fatty fish under Adam,
my wings pinned back. For punishment
God banished me and turned my sister into bone,
honed away everything she'd been
when we lay together among stars.

Some nights I wait at the edge of the garden—
how lush it is, how full of anguish.
Light and docile, she walks toward me,
a trail of creatures at her side.
Does she know I'm here? She's forgotten

my face, forgotten our one smell
as we wound around each other,
her fingers in my mouth, my hand
holding her heartbeat, a wounded wren
I cannot save from grief.

2. The Fall of Eve

When the animals used to talk to me—
lisp of snail, click of grasshopper's
exact consonant—there were rumours
a woman with wings roamed the wasteland.
They said she was furred, sleek and shimmering
as a weasel, eyes wells of desert water
where you'd surely drown.

Not knowing what she feared, I washed
the smell of man from my skin,
walked to where the garden stopped
and everything Adam couldn't name
fell into poetry and silence.

Beside the hawthorn hedge, the forbidden
tart on my tongue, I said *Lilith*
though I didn't remember
what it meant, then I said *Beloved*
and something like a breath lifted
the hair on the back of my neck.

Before I could turn, God's voice
roared through the leaves
and I glimpsed her wings unfolding,
feathers bewildering the sky.
My own arms rose and I know
the way you know your own sorrow
on this earth, once I was that dear,
that close to her,
once I too could fly.

The Sacrifice of Isaac

I bind my breasts with hide. Eat a jackal's heart
and ride in dust to the mountains of Moriah.
Three nights I sit with what they cannot see
beyond their fires. Though I'm close enough
to touch his cheek, I will my hands to stillness.
Before dawn, our last day on the road, a caravan
stutters by, heavy with its load like something
from the past. I am too old for them to trouble me
though a boy rides up, tips his goatskin
and offers me a drink. He drops his eyes
when I unveil my mouth, the darkness there.
I swallow his breath with water from his father's well,
mumble a blessing though I do not know
his gods, their indifference or their lust.
When the groan of wheels fades, I hear
my child's laugh ringing through the grass
like bells tied to the morning wind.
He is climbing. Bent double under wood,
he bears his fire upon his back.
I wait by a thicket, tufts of ram's wool
on the brambles, knife cold against my thigh,
until the altar's built, Isaac asking,
Father, where's the lamb?
then I step into the open, fists on fire,
above my swinging arm
the bare throat of my husband's
Lord opening in a flood of crimson light.

Afterword

See How Many Ends This Stick Has
A Reflection On Poetry

In Wales, a country famous for its singers, my maternal grandfather must
have been a good one. As a young man, before he immigrated to a farm
in Saskatchewan, he sang for his first beer of the day in one of the local
pubs. Perhaps he wasn't melodious enough to get a second, a third, or a
fourth. Those were provided by his horse.

It worked this way: my grandfather didn't allow himself to down his
first beer, bought with a song. He had to have faith like the thirsty man
who pours out the solitary bucket of water to prime a pump, believing
the sacrifice will pay off in a fresh stream gushing from the spout. When
Grandpa raised his pint, his horse, tied up outside, poked his head
through the window, stuck his muzzle in the beer, and guzzled it down,
his master feigning surprise and outrage. The patrons were so delighted
they kept the drinks coming for the man and the horse until closing time
when the two would stumble home in the dark. Grandpa said he didn't
know who was the shakier on his legs. Some nights he thought he'd have
to carry the horse on his back.

My first published poem, "Old Man with a Cane," was about my
grandfather. It wasn't very good—you can tell from the title, but it was
about something I both knew and didn't know well. Although at twenty-
four I was naive about many aspects of writing, my instincts were reliable,
in at least one regard. I didn't write about what I was sure of. Instead, I
struggled with the gap between how my grandfather appeared to me,
the character he became in the few stories he told, and how my mother
perceived him. As a kid, if she hadn't done the chores exactly as he'd
wanted, he went after her with a willow switch, she squirming on her
belly into the farthest corner under the bed as he lashed at her bare legs.
How could that be the same man who let me ride with him on the trac-
tor, who showed me how to make a whistle from a caragana pod, who
sang for his beer with his horse? There was simply something about my

grandfather that resisted language, and resistance is often the place where poetry starts.

I believed then that I'd be able to articulate what I was wrestling with. Now, I know it's not the task of poetry to find the answer. Instead, as Rilke suggested, I've learned to live the questions. To circle what can't be said until something of its smell, sound, taste, and gesture appears on the page. It's as if the body of what I don't know is already out there. Warm-blooded and muscled, it's watching from the trees. I feel its gaze, the unnamed spot on the back of my neck prickles, but I don't see it. I stand patiently on the trail, sometimes seeing a tuft of hair, the small leftover bones of prey, a smudged paw print filling with rain. What's there in the trees has already begun to write itself. My task can be compared to finding the exact chemical substance—the right combination of the senses, the heart, and the intellect—to brush across the page so that the invisible ink of its words can be seen.

Can this be true? Is a writer of such minor importance? Part of me resists this secondary role I've assigned myself because I love the tasks of revising, of refining and extending the metaphor, of fine-tuning the lines, of deleting obscurities and trickery, of finding the most precise word to say what I can't say any other way, of making the language sing. The poem is in the details and I work hard to get them right. Yet however successful or unsuccessful I am, the tasks I've just described come *after* the first words are there. When I'm not writing poetry, what I miss is not what you might expect. I don't mourn the loss of putting the lines on paper, the absence of pages of poems piling up on my desk. I miss the attentiveness that poems demand, the bargain I must make with the world to persuade the words to walk out of the shadows where their lairs are.

When the poem is about to nudge its way into life, when it's pausing on the border between silence and being, it's as if your whole body has grown antennae. As Rumi writes, *You're in your body like a plant is solid on the ground, / yet you're the wind.* The light itself particularizes around you. You notice the graceful way it slides past the rounded corners of the old stove in the kitchen and how it turns into hammered gold in the aspen leaves. It's the same wind that's been blowing all week, but suddenly you sense that it's trying to get a word in and that the long grasses in the ditches refuse to hear. You know, without doubt, this is not your imagination leading you to strange anthropomorphic inventions. You're finally seeing and hearing what is really there, the things that have been going on forever.

〜

There's a courtesy to the kind of attention poetry requires, and what can only be called a devotion. It's a way of honouring all that is outside the self, even though it's the self that filters the sensory details every object and living creature emits. You come across this kind of respect for the Other in many of the haiku masters' small gems. Consider these three lines by Buson:

> A snail,
> one horn short, one long,
> what's on his mind?

I love the unanswerable question and the remarkable distance the poem must cross to take the reader from the second to the third line, but what I delight in just as much is the image I have of the writer: a grown man down on his knees, perhaps prone on his belly, peering at a snail so closely that he notices the tiny lucent horns and marks their difference. He has to see that one is long and one short, simply *see* it, before he can ask his amazing question. It's no accident that the spelling and pronunciation of *see-er* and *seer* are almost the same.

The American poet Robert Hass reminds us of an old Chinese saying: *poetry is like being alive twice*. One of the things this statement refers to is the intensity that paying attention brings to a writer's life. When you're that alert, it's as if time doubles, even as it moves by fast. The moment deepens; you feel what's beneath your feet and what stretches far above your head. The past is here and so is the future. You are in your body, but the borders of your skin that separate you from the air, the sky, and the light, are erased. When you touch a tree, the tree touches back. When you meet the eyes of a fox you travel to his inner eye and he to yours, and nothing keeps you apart. For once, your human language doesn't get in the way.

What a blessing it is, this being alive twice. How could you not want to go on, all of your nerves close to your skin, no matter what the cost? You see, taste, smell, hear, and touch things once—the translucent antennae of a snail, the red comma that is the seed of a Japanese maple, the huge croak of a tree frog who turns out to be smaller than an apricot in your hand. And then you get to experience all of that again in the small charged world of the poem. There's the image, and then there's the image finding its way into words. You get a chance to relive the experience, you go deeper, and if you're lucky, you capture the ephemeral significance of what would otherwise be lost.

And so many things get lost. Not just a set of keys or a photograph of your father with his first truck, but the door those keys once opened, the childhood house you long ago walked into, the father who used to carry you on his shoulders high above the crowds at the summer fair, his body now ashes and shards of bone. You hold these things in place on a page, you walk through that door, touch his face and smell the cigarette smoke on his breath and in his shirt, you make things breathe again in words. You feel the lightness of a ghostly touch across your skin. In that small house on the corner, the porch light suddenly comes on.

~

See how many ends this stick has! Montaigne wrote in the sixteenth century. That imperative has become a motto, one of the things I strive to do—to look at the ordinary until I observe what is truly there but extraordinarily so because I'm seeing it (hearing it, smelling it) for the first time and, as far as I know, no one else has written the insight down. Covered with hoarfrost, this stick has a dozen ends, not two! Why didn't I see that before?

For years I'd wanted to write about gophers, but they've been popping their heads out of so many books that I thought every gopher-like nuance known to humankind had been recorded. The word itself in prairie literature has come close to being a cliché. Then luckily for me two unrelated things converged. I was in the middle of revisiting Old Testament stories for the manuscript that would become *Apocrypha of Light*, and for a couple of years, everything I looked at fell into a religious context. Gophers, I thought, are as unappreciated on the prairies as prophets in their own country. They've been poisoned, drowned, shot, and burnt alive in stubble fields. My mother ripped off their tails when she was a child and sold them for a penny a piece to the elevator agent as proof that she'd successfully done away with them. Pondering their role as victims, I went for my daily walk down the country road that bordered the place where I was staying. I stopped a few feet away from a gopher standing upright by his burrow at the edge of a field. Here was a creature I'd been looking at all my life—the most ubiquitous animal on the prairies— and I was suddenly startled by the beauty of his ears. How small, curved and flat they were, how perfectly formed for an animal who had been designed to dig head first into the dirt. And what about that action, that going blindly down into darkness? The number of the ends of this stick is rapidly increasing! The gopher is both what he is and something more, something I was beginning to see and intuit before the poem began to break out of silence: *I come to him with questions / because I love his ears.*

~

Music and poetry—the words are interchangeable. *There is a song in everything*, the wise ones say. Words of course carry meaning but so does their sound, a resonance that hums in our bones. Consider this small scenario: Thomas Edison is standing in the room with a piano and pianist, ready to make the first recording on his new invention. Music fills the air, his memory machine starts trapping the sound, but deaf, he can't hear a thing. Out of his mind with frustration, he rushes to the piano and bites the corner, locking his mouth and teeth on the cherry wood so he can feel the vibrations and "hear" the recording. I want to hear like that; I want to hear like Beethoven, I want to hear like my fellow countryman, John Newlove, who wrote, *Ride off any horizon / and let the measure fall / where it may.* That combustible combination of sight and sound he lit upon. We bite the corner of the big sky we were born under so the small bones of the inner ear vibrate with that vast blue measure and we bring it softly down.

In his various writings, Barry Lopez reminds us that the land is speaking; we just have to learn to listen. What are the vast plains of my childhood saying? How do they sound? In a 2004 Canada Day interview on CBC Radio, the singer k.d. lang claimed that growing up on the Alberta prairies influenced her voice. The huge distances and minimalism led to her long tones, the vibrato held back till the last moment. She said there's so much horizon, that she learned to sing loudly, to reach out far. Consul, Alberta, where she grew up, had no concert hall or theatre, but like every small town on the prairies, it had a curling rink, a long narrow building with a low curved roof. She'd ride to the rink on her motorcycle, her small dog sitting on the gas tank, and in the summer when no one was inside, she'd slip in and sing, her voice sliding down the length of what in winter would be sheets of ice, her notes reverberating in that empty hollow and echoing back.

I wish I had a comparable story about my voice being shaped by the place I still call home. I know from having heard myself read poems on the radio that I draw out my vowels in a Midwestern way. Is that local accent influenced by the long stretch of road and sky? I hope, like k.d. lang, that my poems are reaching far, but that's for someone else to judge, not me. I want to draw that unbroken undulating landscape into the poem without caging it, without crowding it around the edges. At the very least, I want my poems to keep the windows open so that a good wind can blow through.

The sheer enormity of where I come from resists words, but as I said at the start, poetry often begins with such resistance. How can the small letters you compose, standing as tall as possible on any page, make themselves visible in a landscape that diminishes the human? At the same time, the place demands that you keep your eyes and ears open because the space around you feels attenuated, on the verge, ready to reveal its meaning in the blink of an eye. It duplicates the feeling you get just before the curtain is about to open in a theatre, just before the violinist's bow is about to meet the strings in a concert hall. Every single stone on the gravel road has its own shadow, sharply defined. Long before you hear any thunder, you can see the weather coming at you from miles away, lightning striding over the fields from the East, clear sky above you, the dark veils of rain draping the southwest corner. With your whole being you sense that something is about to happen. It could be a grouse taking off with your heart as it explodes from the bush in front of you or the sudden annunciation of a huge, flat-bottomed cumulus that drapes you in shadow. It could be an angel formed from all the light pouring off the roof and sides of a tin Quonset. Is that what the dog sees? Is that the cause of its barking?

Standing under a sky so blue it would ring if you threw a penny up into the air, you feel yourself vibrate like a tuning fork. The impossibility of translating the place, the people (your grandfather, your father, the first boy you loved), your soon-to-be-over life, seduces you into language. Maybe this time I'll get closer, you think, to what predates speaking, to what tantalizes you with all that can't be named.

—*Lorna Crozier*

Acknowledgements

From *Humans and Other Beasts*
Winnipeg: Turnstone, 1980
    Still-Life [reprinted in *The Garden Going On Without Us*]

From *The Garden Going On Without Us*
Toronto: McClelland and Stewart, 1985
    Still-Life
    Poem about Nothing
    This Is a Love Poem without Restraint
    The Child Who Walks Backwards
    Carrots
    Onions

From *Angels of Flesh, Angels of Silence*
Toronto: McClelland and Stewart, 1988
    Fear of Snakes
    Quitting Smoking
    The Goldberg Variations
    Home Town
    Male Thrust
    Mother and I, Walking
    How to Stop Missing Your Friend Who Died

From *Inventing the Hawk*
Toronto: McClelland and Stewart, 1992
    On the Seventh Day
    Living Day by Day
    Angel of Bees
    Canada Day Parade

From *Everything Arrives at the Light*
Toronto: McClelland and Stewart, 1995
    The Dark Ages of the Sea
    The Red Onion in Skagway, Alaska
    The Wild Boys
    The Garden at Night
    Going Back

From *A Saving Grace: The Collected Poems of Mrs. Bentley*
Toronto: McClelland and Stewart, 1996
    Dust
    The Kind of Woman
    Not the Music
    Mrs Bentley

From *What the Living Won't Let Go*
Toronto: McClelland and Stewart, 1999
    Packing for the Future: Instructions
    Watching My Lover
    What You Remember Remains
    A Kind of Love
    Wildflowers

From *Apocrypha of Light*
Toronto: McClelland and Stewart, 2002
    The Origin of the Species
    What the Snake Brings to the World
    Original Sin (1 & 2)
    The Sacrifice of Isaac